SKATEBOARDS

MADE BY HAND

SKATEBOARDS

BY PATRICIA LAKIN

ALADDIN

New York   London   Toronto   Sydney   New Delhi

For Lee, Aaron, and Benjahmin because you each, in your own way, put wheels under my feet and help me fly

ALADDIN

An imprint of Simon & Schuster Children's Publishing Division
1230 Avenue of the Americas, New York, New York 10020
First Aladdin hardcover edition February 2017
Text copyright © 2017 by Simon & Schuster, Inc.
Cover photograph of skateboard copyright © 2017 by Jake Eshelman
All other cover photographs and illustrations copyright © Thinkstock
Photographs of skateboards on pages 2, 3, and 7, photograph of leather pieces on
page 24, and featured photographs on pages 8, 9, 11, 12, 13, 14, 15, 16, 17, 18, 19, 20,
21, 22, 23, 24, and 25 copyright © 2017 by Jake Eshelman
Photograph of skateboarders on page 28 copyright © 2017 Bettmann/CORBIS
Photograph of skateboarders on page 29 copyright © 2017 Tequask via Wikimedia Commons
Side Project Skateboards logo on page 23 is a trademark of Jake Eshelman
All other interior photographs and illustrations © Thinkstock
For information about special discounts for bulk purchases, please contact Simon & Schuster
Special Sales at 1-866-506-1949 or business@simonandschuster.com.
The Simon & Schuster Speakers Bureau can bring authors to your live event.
For more information or to book an event, contact the Simon & Schuster Speakers Bureau at
1-866-248-3049 or visit our website at www.simonspeakers.com.
Book designed by Lissi Erwin / SPLENDID CORP.
The text of this book was set in Univers LTD, Haneda, and AG Book Stencil.
Manufactured in China 1116 SCP
10 9 8 7 6 5 4 3 2 1
Library of Congress Cataloging-in-Publication Data
Names: Lakin, Patricia, 1944– author.
Title: Skateboards / by Patricia Lakin.
Description: First Aladdin hardcover edition. | New York : Aladdin, [2017] |
Series: Made by Hand ; 1 | Audience: Ages: 8-12. | Audience: Grades: 4 to 6.
Identifiers: LCCN 2016016442 | ISBN 9781481448338 (paper over board) |
    ISBN 9781481448345 (eBook)
Subjects: LCSH: Skateboarding—History—Juvenile literature. |
    Skateboards—Design and construction—Juvenile literature. | Board books.
Classification: LCC GV859.8 .L35 2017 | DDC 796.2209—dc23
LC record available at https://lccn.loc.gov/2016016442

IF YOU'VE GOT WHEELS UNDER YOUR FEET, YOU CAN

fly.

WHAT FREEDOM! You can swoosh on a skateboard.

You can use it for tricks or for travel.

Just what is a skateboard? In the following pages you'll find out. You'll also get a behind-the-scenes look at a very special company where these wheeled wonders are *made by hand*. You'll find out why the man who created this busi-

put wheels under his

WHAT IS A SKATEBOARD?

TRUCKS

WHEEL

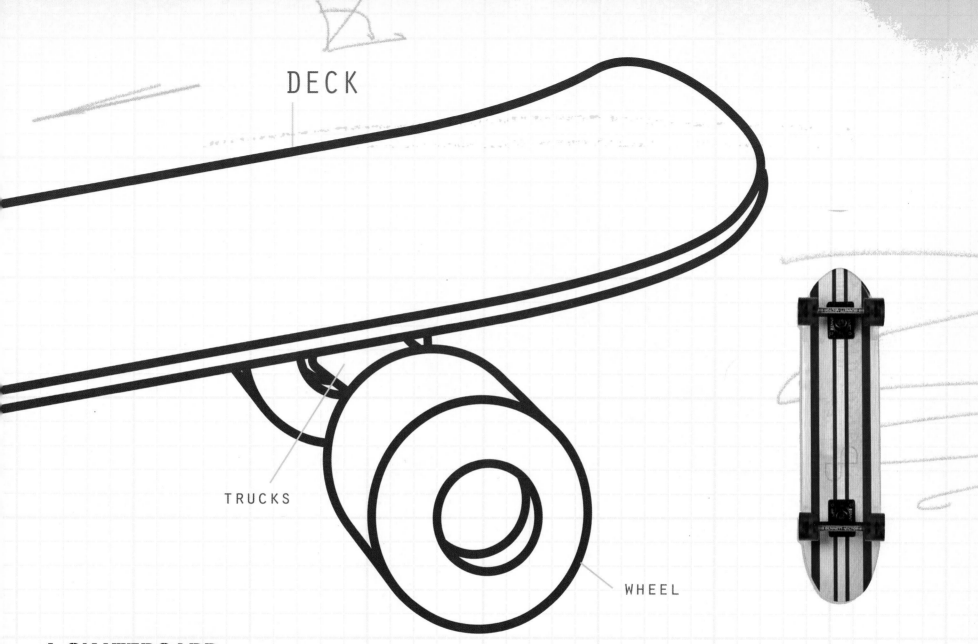

DECK

TRUCKS

WHEEL

A SKATEBOARD is a narrow board. It has four wheels attached to its underside. There are three main parts. There is the deck or top part—the part you put your feet on! The trucks are the metal pieces attached underneath. They hold the third part, the wheels.

But a skateboard is so much more than its parts.

HISTORY OF THE SKATEBOARD

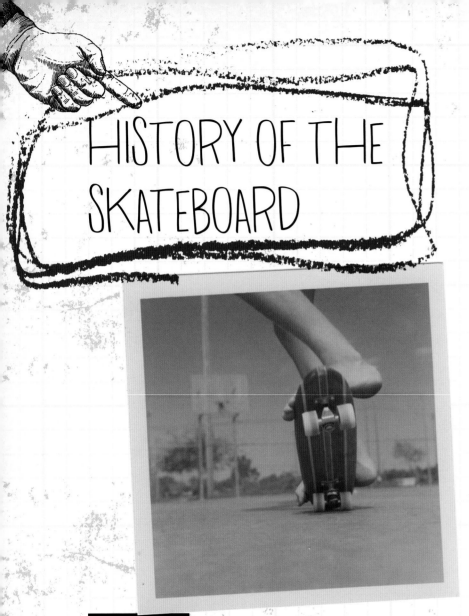

Most people would pick California as the birthplace of skateboards. That's because there's a strong link between skateboarding and surfing. But California surfers could ride the waves only when there *were* waves! When the Pacific Ocean was calm, those surfers needed another way to keep their bodies moving!

In the 1960s these itching-to-go surfers would make their own skateboards. First they'd find a plank of wood. Then they would take the wheels off roller skates and nail them onto their board. Presto! They had their own skateboard. Soon the sport spread far beyond California.

NO ONE really knows who made the first skateboard. But kids longed to have wheels under their feet. Even before the 1920s kids nailed a wooden fruit crate onto a board, attached wheels to it, and took off! By the 1930s companies were making scooter-style metal boards.

CALIFORNIA, USA

The next thirty years brought improvements in the wheels and the boards' decks. In 1972 a company named Cadillac created wheels made of a material called urethane. These wheels gripped the sidewalk surface and gave skateboarders a smoother ride. And instead of a straight slab of wood, many decks now have a raised front and/or back lip. This allows the rider to do more skating tricks.

Over time skateboarders kept coming up with new and interesting ways to use the board. Now special parks are constructed to give skateboarders places to ride. Some skateboard designers want to make boards that help skateboarders try new tricks. Other designers want to bring back the beauty found in old-style boards.

That's where Jake Eshelman comes in. He started a company called Side Project Skateboards. He purposely makes his boards flat, to honor the style of the sixties. Most important for Jake, he can proudly say, "My skateboards are made by me. They are all made by hand."

Meet Jake Eshelman

WHOOOSH! Eight-year-old Jake Eshelman swooped downhill on his snowboard. He loved this winter sport but couldn't do it often. Jake grew up in Virginia. There are no high mountains in Virginia, and there's not much snow.

His mom suggested he get a skateboard. Yes! Whizzing on that board gave Jake the same joy and thrill as snowboarding. And he could do it year-round.

Jake kept on skateboarding even when he went off to college in San Antonio, Texas. Jake was sure he'd go on to law school. His plans changed after he met and fell in love with a classmate, Margaux. She was an art major. Jake got to learn about Margaux's artistic world and realized he could have a career creating things. He gave up the idea of law school.

After college they both moved to Houston, Margaux's hometown. Jake started working with Margaux's father, Hugh. He frames pieces of art.

As the two worked side by side, Hugh filled Jake with stories of his own skateboarding adventures from when Hugh was growing up in the sixties. Hugh's stories gave Jake, still a dedicated skateboarder, an idea. Each day Jake had to toss out beautiful strips of maple, swamp ash, cherry, or walnut. They were too small to use for the art frames Hugh made. But Jake was drawn to the variety of colors and the magnificent patterns in those wood strips. What if Jake glued them together? He could make his very own skateboard.

That's what Jake did! Skating on a board made with his own hands gave Jake a feeling of joy. In fact, it is

JAKE SNOWBOARDING AS A KID

JAKE SKATEBOARDING IN COLLEGE

HERE IS JAKE WITH THE FIRST SKATEBOARD HE EVER BUILT!

still the board that Jake uses every day as he skateboards around town. Others saw Jake's board and wanted one too. And that's how Side Project Skateboards was born.

Making skateboards is Jake's side project. His other career is in creative advertising. He helps other companies sell their products. Jake deals with words and ideas all day long.

In the evening he enters his woodworking shop and he turns on the heavy metal music that he loves.

Then he gets to work. Making something with his very own hands gives Jake such a sense of accomplishment that it's almost impossible to describe. The skills he uses in his day job help him tell people online and in the real world all about Side Project Skateboards.

The advice Jake would like to pass on is,

"BE HONEST WITH YOURSELF. FIND WHAT FIRES YOUR PASSION. ABOVE ALL, FEEL COMFORTABLE AND UNAFRAID TO TAKE CHANCES."

JAKE'S IPOD—HE MADE THE CASE!

JAKE'S STUDIO IN HOUSTON, TEXAS, ON A HOT SUMMER DAY

JAKE'S FATHER-IN-LAW IN THE 1960S

HOW THE SKATEBOARD IS MADE

JAKE goes through Hugh's pile of tossed-out wood strips. He prefers using hardwoods such as maple, cherry, and walnut. He looks at the wood's color and the designs that the wood's lines or grains make. For some steps Jake uses his hands. For others, to save time, he uses machines. From start to finish, including drying time, it takes Jake approximately one week to make a skateboard.

Walk into Jake's large gray-floored work space, and you'll see wood of every size and color! Wide wood planks and tall narrow strips lean against one wall. Nearby is an L-shaped wooden worktable. A white Peg-Board holds wrenches, pincers, scrapers, and tape measures. Hanging vacuum hoses are ready to suck up the curly wood chips that will fall to the floor.

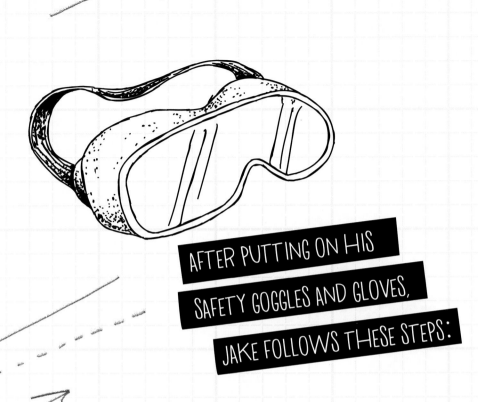

AFTER PUTTING ON HIS SAFETY GOGGLES AND GLOVES, JAKE FOLLOWS THESE STEPS:

STEP 1: He chooses strips of wood based on their color and grains and puts them out on a big table. At this point the strips are not all the same length or thickness. He decides which strips look good together. He arranges them to form a pattern.

STEP 2: He examines each strip to make sure it is strong and has no cracks or splits.

15

STEP 3: He places those strips on their flat side on a table and sands down the long sides of each strip.

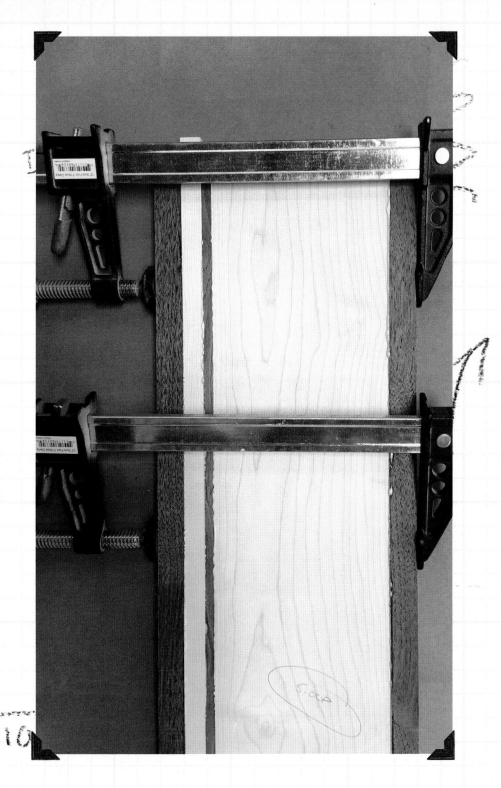

STEP 4: He makes sure these "inner" sides fit together. Then he glues the strips to one another, puts a clamp on them to hold them that way, and lets them dry overnight.

STEP 5: Jake uses a saw called a planer to make both sides of the board totally flat. He shaves down his skateboards so they are five-eighths-inch thick.

STEP 6: He sands down the board so that it is perfectly flat on both sides.

STEP 7: Jake uses a thirty-inch-long clear plastic pattern, or template, to cut out the skateboard shape from the wood he has sanded, glued, and planed. The clear plastic template lets him see the deck's wood colors and grains through it. He decides just where he should cut out the skateboard. (He doesn't want to cut away an especially beautiful part of the wood.)

STEP 8: He traces around the template with a pencil. With a band saw he cuts out the board along the pencil lines.

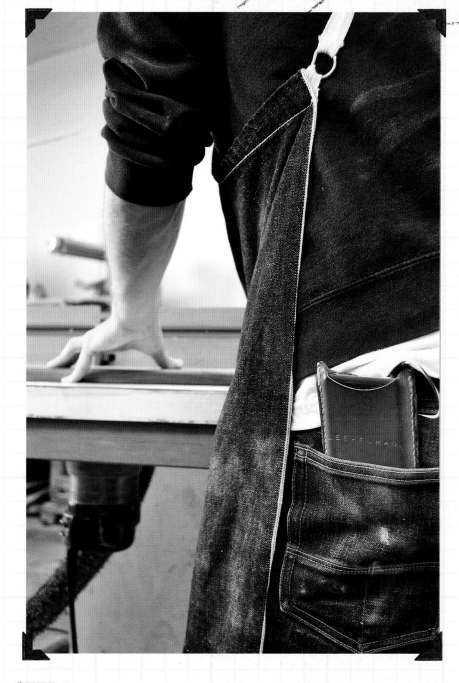

STEP 9: Jake uses a tool called a router to round all the edges on the board. (The rounded edges make the board easier to ride and to hold.)

19

STEP 10: Jake then sands the edges down by hand to make sure they are perfectly smooth.

STEP 11: He takes another template and puts it on the underside of the board. This helps him mark where the wheel wells will go. (The wheels should never hit the underside of the board. The wheel wells allow the rider to tilt the board without it hitting the wheel.)

STEP 13: OOOOPS! When Jake first started making skateboards, his hand slipped when he was doing the third wheel well. He'd accidentally made a swirl, like a fish tail. Hmm. Jake liked the look. He turned his mistake around. He now makes that swirl mark near the back wheels on all of his skateboards. It's his unofficial signature.

STEP 12: Then Jake uses a belt sander to make the four small rounded grooves or wheel wells in the underside of the wood.

STEP 15: Jake puts oil on both sides of the board. This oil makes the wood's color and grains really stand out, or "pop."

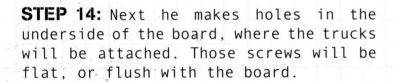

STEP 14: Next he makes holes in the underside of the board, where the trucks will be attached. Those screws will be flat, or flush with the board.

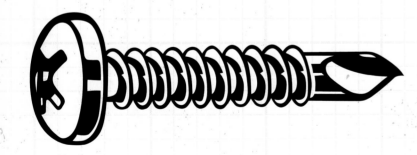

STEP 16: Then Jake puts a waterproof varnish over the entire board and lets it dry. This takes from three to six days, depending on how damp or dry the weather is.

STEP 17: Jake takes the board to a laser studio where his company's official logo is cut into the board's varnish on its underside.

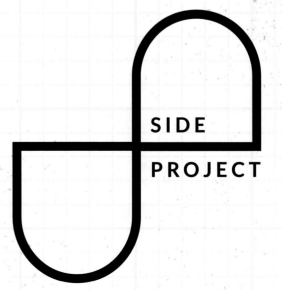

SIDE
PROJECT

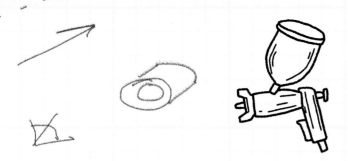

STEP 18: Then Jake sprays the top of the deck of his board with very finely crushed glass. This final coating makes it easier for the rider to grip the board with his or her feet *and* allows the beautiful wood to shine through.

STEP 19: **FINALLY,** Jake cuts out two small pieces of leather, which he places between the trucks and the wooden underside of the board. The leather absorbs shock for a smoother ride. He attaches the trucks and wheels.

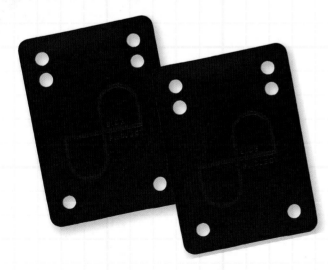

JAKE'S SIDE PROJECT SKATEBOARD,
MADE BY HAND, WITH LOVE AND CARE,
IS READY TO RIDE!

NOW IT'S YOUR TURN

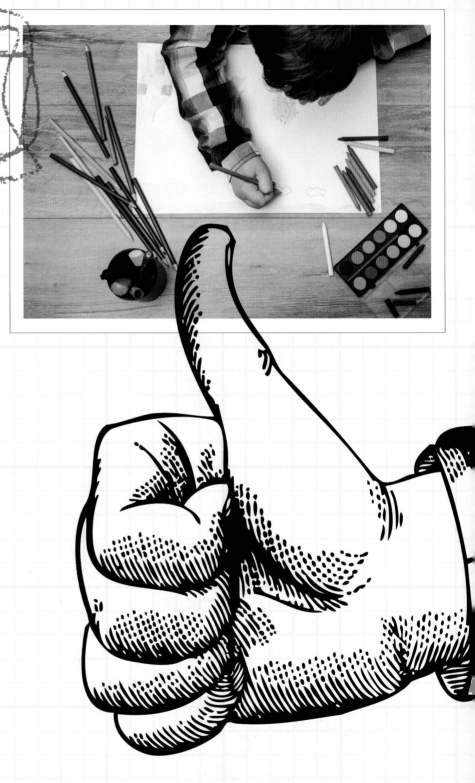

Jake is passionate about what he does—making something with his very own hands. He believes that a handmade object is extra special. A real person used his or her own skills and care to make that object.

Have you ever been given something that was made by hand? Was it a drawing or made from clay? Was it sewn or knitted? Was it made from wood, or pasta, or papier-mâché?

Have you ever made something by hand? If you have, do you remember the great feeling of accomplishment you had when you were done? That feeling is especially wonderful if you've made your object as a gift.

If you've never made something with your hands, why not give it a try? There is no end to what you can make. The choices are as gigantic as your imagination. Make something brand-new. Or use objects that are about to be thrown out. Let your creative juices flow! How can you turn a bottle cap or a paper plate or an empty spool of thread into something brand-new?

Got an idea? Great! You'll be creating something with your own hands—and recycling!

Recycling? Did you know that skateboards can be recycled? You can get a fixed-up skateboard. Or you can pass yours on to someone who would love to put wheels under their own feet.

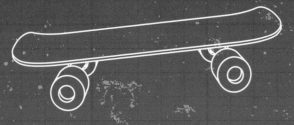

SKATEBOARD TIME LINE

1920s—Kids nail a wooden fruit crate to a narrow wooden board and attach roller skate wheels to the front and back.

1930s—A metal rocket-shaped three-wheeled scooter called a "scooter-skate" is made.

1940s—A company makes a four-wheeled aluminum scooter-type skateboard.

1950s—Kids, especially Californians, put "wheels under their feet" by nailing roller skate wheels to a plank of wood.

1962—A California surfboard shop, Val Surf, makes skateboards using a roller skate company's wheels. This new sport is called "sidewalk surfing."

1963—Larry Stevenson designs skateboards and uses clay wheels.

1965—The National Skateboard Championships are held in Anaheim, California, and are broadcast on ABC's *Wide World of Sports*.

1966—Surfer's World, a skateboard park, opens in Anaheim, California.

1969—Larry Stevenson designs a skateboard he calls the "kicktail." The front and back parts of the deck are tipped up slightly.

1972—A group of Southern California teenagers form a team called the Zephyrs. They base their unique skating style on surfers' moves.

1972—Frank Nasworthy makes urethane wheels just for skateboards. He calls his company Cadillac.

1974—The United States Skateboard Association is formed, bringing together skateboarders from around the country.

1976–1978—The California drought leaves swimming pools empty. The Zephyrs use these empty pools and create a new skating move known as Vert, for vertical skating.

1978—A Zephyr team member, Alan "Ollie" Gelfand, invents a skating move. With feet on the board, the skater lifts the board into the air. This move is called the ollie.

1986—The Trans World Skateboard Championships are held in Vancouver, Canada.

OLLIE

2001—A documentary about the Zephyr team debuts. It's called *Dogtown and Z-Boys*. (Dogtown is the area in Southern California where the Z-Boys hung out.)

2004—June 21, 2004, becomes the first Go Skateboarding Day, started by the International Association of Skateboard Companies.

2007—Skateistan, a nonprofit organization, is founded to encourage children in Afghanistan to build leadership skills through skateboarding. www.skateistan.org

2010—I Ride I Recycle is an organization that collects reusable and broken skateboards through participating skate shops. Their goal is to keep old boards out of landfills. Kids can get a used board. Broken boards are given to Art of Board and used as wall coverings or other art projects. www.irideirecycle.com | artofboard.com

GLOSSARY & RESOURCES

DECK: The top of a skateboard where the rider stands.

LIP: The upturned edge of a skateboard.

LOGO: The design a business or company creates to identify itself.

TEMPLATE: A pattern or mold that is used as a guide when cutting out an object.

TOOLS:

BAND SAW: A machine with a thin, oval saw blade.

PLANER: A machine that scrapes down wood or metal to make it smooth and flat.

PINCERS: A pointy, curved, jaw-like tool that holds thin objects like a nail.

ROUTER: A machine that cuts out rounded or indented edges.

WRENCH: A jaw-like tool that can hold or turn objects thicker than nails.

TRUCK: A metal T-shaped part that attaches to the underside of a skateboard so the wheels can be attached.

WOOD GRAIN: The pattern of lines in a piece of wood.

URETHANE: A man-made plastic-like substance.

VARNISH: A clear liquid coating that is applied to the surface of an object in order to protect the material it's made of.

WEBSITES:

www.skateboardingmagazine.com/the-evolution-of-skateboarding-a-history-from-sidewalk-surfing-to-superstardom/

teacher.scholastic.com/scholasticnews/indepth/Skateboarding/articles/index.asp?article=history&topic=0

www.skateistan.org/content/our-story

www.edutopia.org/video/learning-physics-skateboarding-engages-kids-science

skatopia.org/museum1/

skateboard.about.com/cs/boardscience/a/brief_history.htm

www.exploratorium.edu/skateboarding/skatedesign.html

www.skatewhat.com/russhowell/WebPage-SkateboardHistoryTimeline.html

time.com/3877898/skateboarding-photos-from-the-early-days-of-the-sport-and-the-pastime/

theiasc.org/just-one-board

www.madehow.com/Volume-6/Skateboard.html